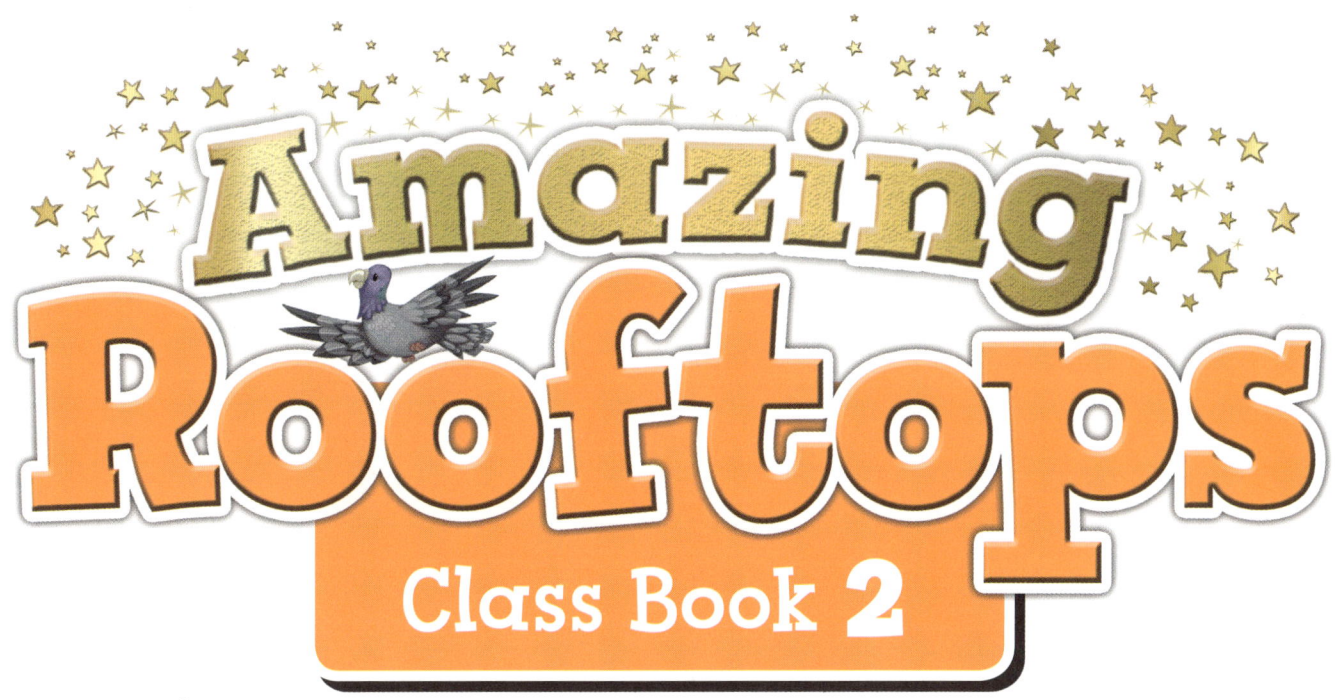

Amazing Rooftops
Class Book 2

Helen Casey

Oscar Anna Nizzy Neena

PARK STREET

OXFORD
UNIVERSITY PRESS

Lesson 1 Vocabulary

Welcome to Rooftops School

1. Listen, point and repeat. 🔊 1
2. Listen and say the next number. 🔊 2
3. Listen and chant. 🔊 3

4. Listen and repeat. 🔊 4

5. Draw. Show and tell.

At school

2 | **Vocabulary** Numbers 11–20 | How are you? I'm fine, thank you.

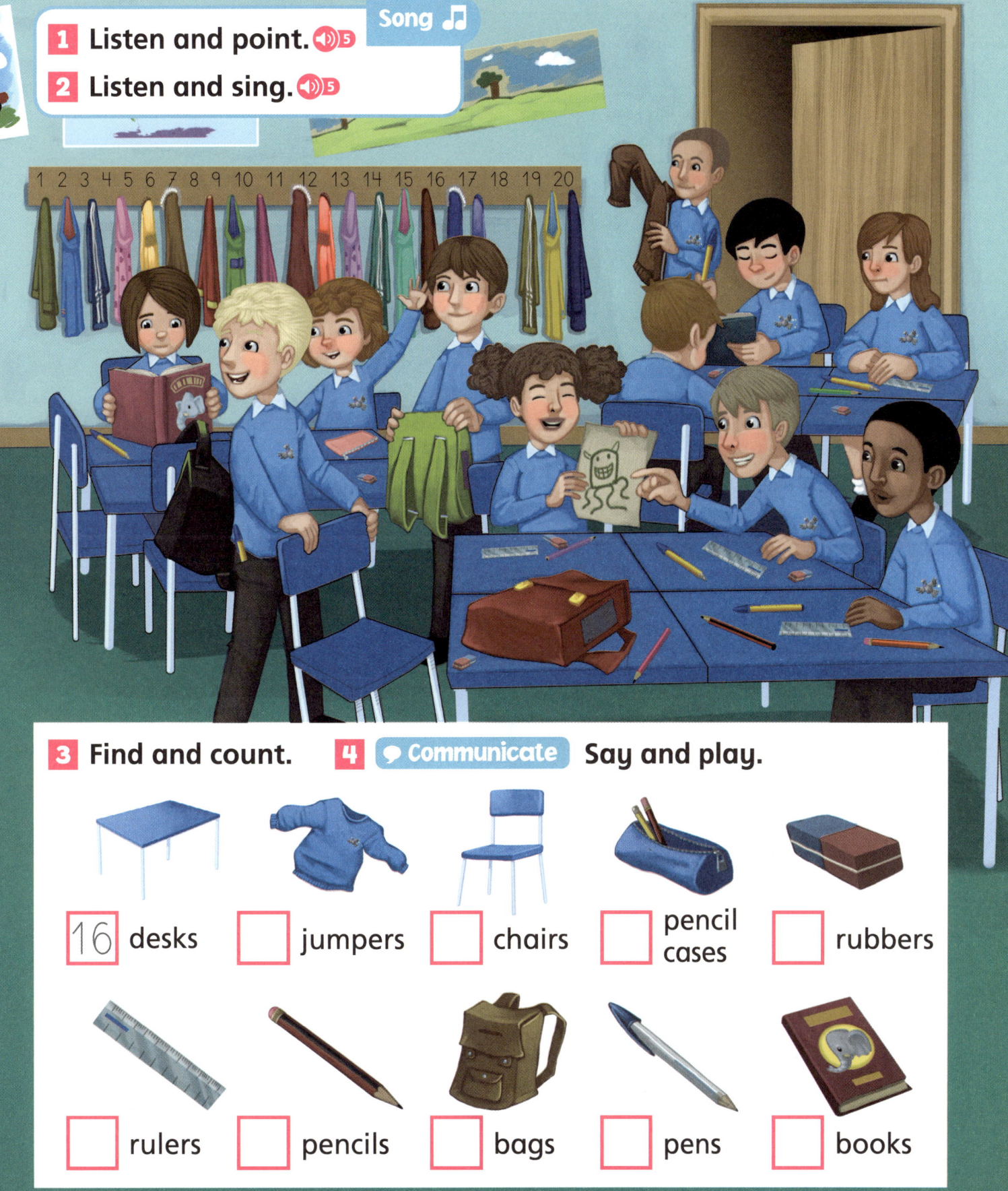

Lesson 3 Vocabulary

1 Listen, point and repeat. 🔊6   **2** Listen and say the word. 🔊7

1 cold   2 rainy   3 snowy
4 hot   5 sunny   6 windy

3 Circle. Listen and number. 🔊8   **4** 💬 Communicate Say and play.

It's (hot) / cold.

It's rainy / snowy.

It's windy / sunny.

It's cold / hot.

It's snowy / sunny.

It's windy / rainy.

Vocabulary the weather

Lesson 4 Vocabulary

1 Listen, point and repeat. 🔊 9   **2** Listen and say the word. 🔊 10

spring

summer

autumn

winter

3 Listen and point. 🔊 11 Listen and sing. 🔊 11

Song 🎵

4 Write and say.

spring
summer
autumn
winter

It's ...

Vocabulary seasons

Lesson 2 Song and Grammar

1 Listen and sing. 🔊16 Listen and number. 🔊17 Write.   Song 🎵

garden _____ _____ _____

_____ _____ _____ _____

2 Listen and match. 🔊18   **3** 💬 Communicate Say and play.

Where's Grandpa?

He's in the kitchen!

Where's ... ? He's / She's in the ...   7

Lesson 3 Culture

At home

1 Look and say the places. Write.

2 Listen and number. 🔊 19

| living room | bedroom |
| kitchen | garden |

3 Make a mini-book. **AB** 💬 **Communicate** Show and tell.

I'm in the bedroom. I've got a ball!

Me, too!

Life skills

Lesson 4 Everyday language and Values **1**

1 Listen and point. 🔊 21   Listen and repeat. 🔊 21

2 Listen, look and match. 🔊 22   Say.

3 💬 Communicate   Act out with your friend.

Can I help?

Yes, please. Thank you.

You're welcome.

Our Values

Do you help at home?

Life skills 9

Lesson 5 Story

Where's Kitty?

1 Listen and follow the story.

1. Kitty? Where's the cat? Kitty!
Come on, Anna. Let's look for Kitty.

2. Where's Kitty?
Look! She's on the sofa!

3. It's a hat!
Where's Kitty?

4. Listen! She's in the cupboard.
Oh! Poor Kitty.
No, it's not Kitty.

5. Listen! She's in the bathroom.
Kitty's in the bath!

6. It's my doll!
Where's Kitty?

2 ↻ Review Find and circle. 💬 Communicate Say.

3 Listen and repeat. 🔊 24   💬 Think Colour and say.

I think the story is …

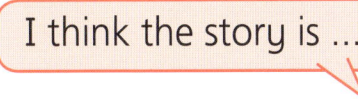

1

Lesson 6 Vocabulary and Grammar

1 Listen, point and repeat. 🔊 25 **Listen and say the word.** 🔊 26

cupboard

bath

bed

table

sofa

2 Listen and say. Who is it? 🔊 27 **Listen and repeat.** 🔊 27

3 💬 Communicate Play.

"He's in the garage. He's in the cupboard!"

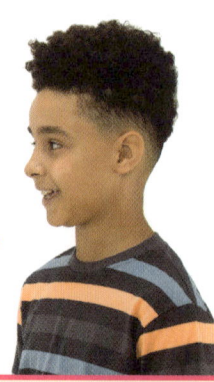
"It's Uncle!"

under / in

on / under

in / on

on / in

Vocabulary furniture   She's / He's in / on / under …

Rooftops Book Club

Lesson 7 Literacy **1**

1 What does Grandpa want to make? Guess and tick ✓.

a cake ☐   eggs ☐   sandwiches ☐   sausages ☐

2 📖 page 4 and 5 🔊 28   Tick ✓ Grandpa's cake.

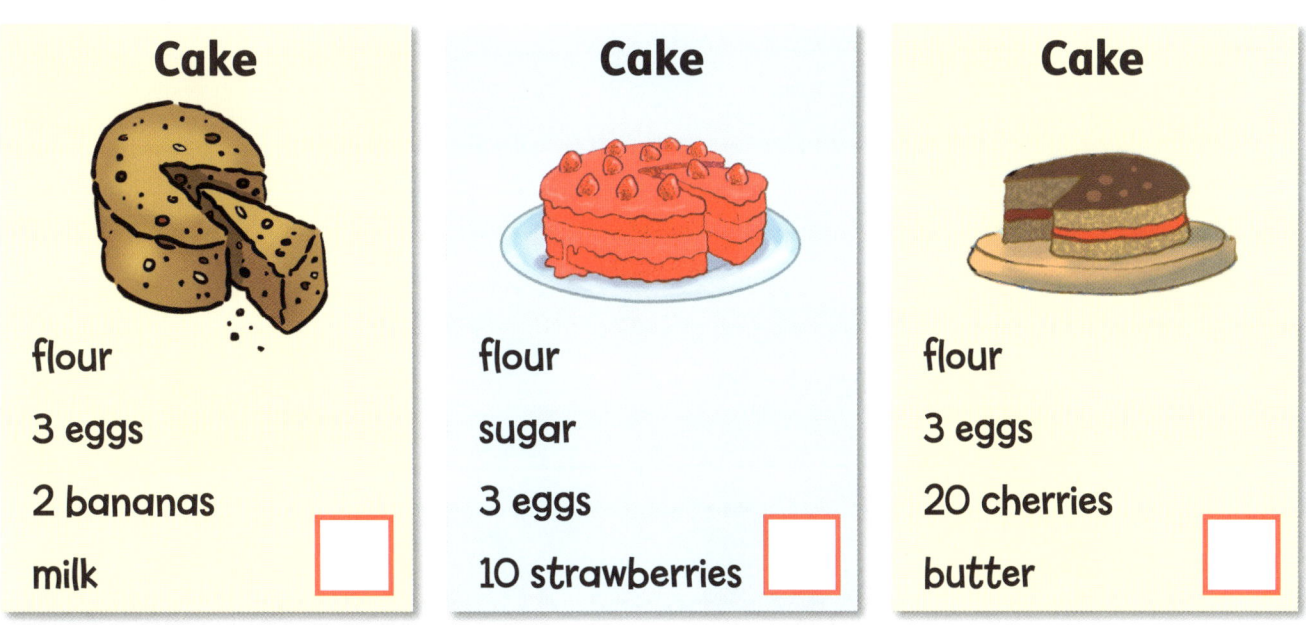

Cake
flour
3 eggs
2 bananas
milk ☐

Cake
flour
sugar
3 eggs
10 strawberries ☐

Cake
flour
3 eggs
20 cherries
butter ☐

3 💬 Communicate   Listen and repeat. 🔊 29   Act out with your friend.

Do you like cake?

Yes, I do.

Literacy reading a story   **13**

Rooftops Skills

Lesson 8 Communication

Listen and Speak

1 Listen and number. 🔊 30 Write *in*, *on*, or *under*. 💬 Communicate Say.

under _____ on _____

in _____ under _____

2 Make your communication cards. **CB page 93**

3 🔷 Collaborate Say and play.

14 Life skills

Rooftops Round Up

Lesson 9 Round Up 1

Song 🎵

1 Listen and point. 🔊 32   Listen and sing. 🔊 32

2 💡 **Be creative**   Listen and read. 🔊 33   Draw and write. Share.

This is my brother.
He's in the bathroom.
He's in the bath.

An amazing hiding place!

This is my _____.

He's / She's _____.

He's / She's _____.

Life skills

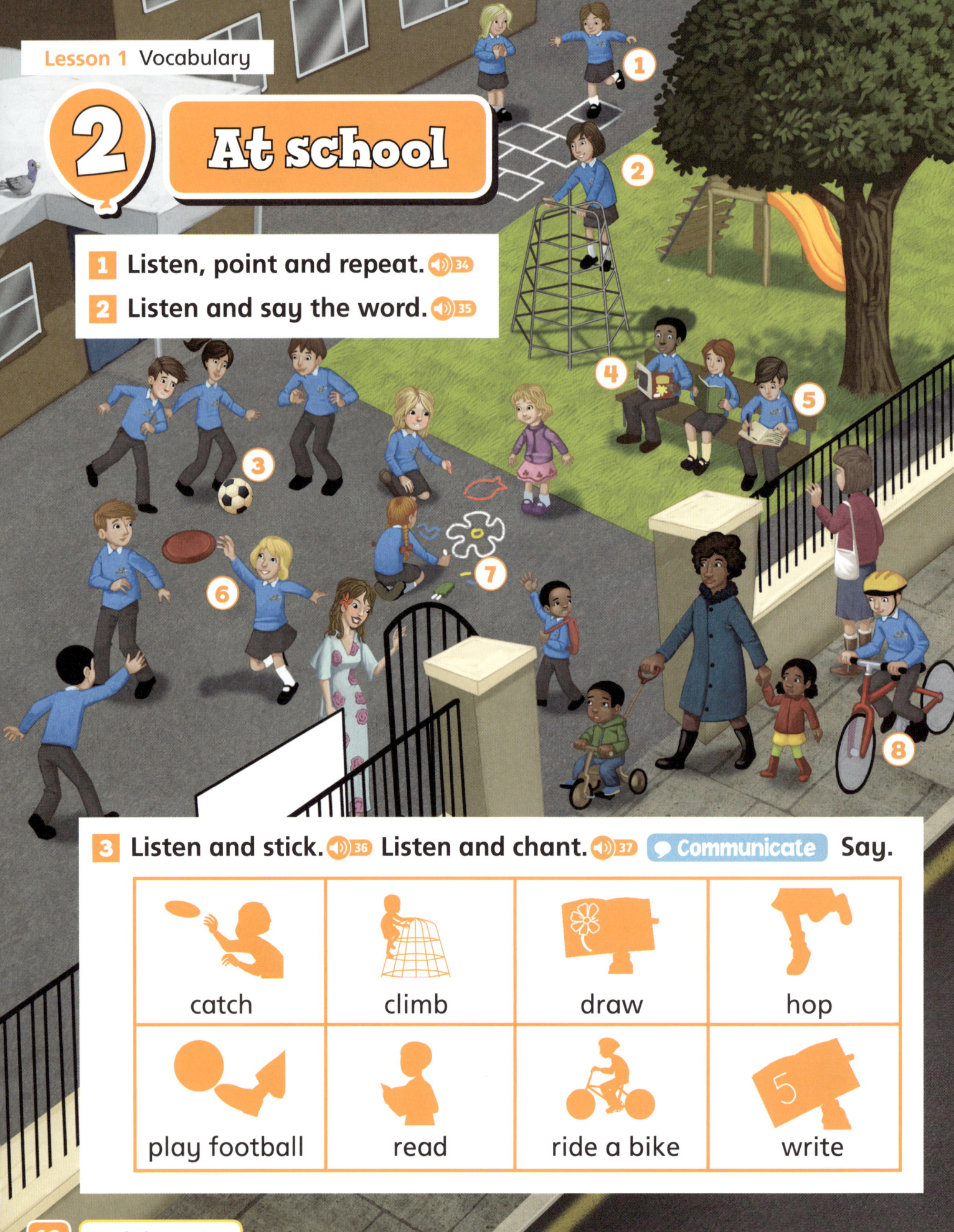

Lesson 2 Song and Grammar

1 Listen and sing. 🔊 38 Listen and number. 🔊 39 Write.

2 Listen and tick ✓ or cross ✗. 🔊 40   **3** 💬 Communicate Say and play.

She can draw.
She can't write.

Number 1!

He / She can't …

2 Lesson 3 Culture — Play time!

1 Look and say the actions. Write.

2 Listen and number. 🔊 41

jump   run   draw   hop

3 Make a mini-book. **AB** 💬 **Communicate** Show and tell.

"This is my friend. She can run."

Life skills

Lesson 4 Everyday language and Values **2**

1 Listen and point. 🔊42 Listen and repeat. 🔊42

2 Listen and number. 🔊43 Write *my* or *your*. Say.

It's my turn.

It's your turn.

It's _____ turn.

It's _____ turn.

3 💬 Communicate Act out with your friend.

Whose turn is it?

It's your turn!

Our Values

Do you take turns?

Life skills 19

2 Lesson 5 Story

Nizzy's surprise

1 Listen and follow the story.

Literacy understanding a story

2 🔄 **Review** Find and circle. 💬 **Communicate** Say.

3 Listen and repeat. 🔊 45 💭 **Think** Colour and say.

I think the story is …

2 Lesson 6 Vocabulary and Grammar

1 Listen, point and repeat. 🔊 46 **Listen and say the word.** 🔊 47

playground

bike shed

toilets

classroom

gym

2 Listen and say the number. 🔊 48 **Listen and repeat.** 🔊 48

3 Communicate   Play.

She can ride a bike.
She isn't in the playground.
She's in the bike shed.

Number 4.

Vocabulary places in a school   He / She's in the … He / She isn't in the …

Rooftops Book Club

Lesson 7 Literacy

1 Who makes the cake? Guess and tick ✓.

Grandpa ☐   Rosie and Ben ☐   Clunk ☐   The Cake Machine ☐

2 📖 page 6 and 7 🔊 49 Order the ingredients. Who puts them in? Write **G** for 👴 or **C** for 🤖. Circle the extra ingredient.

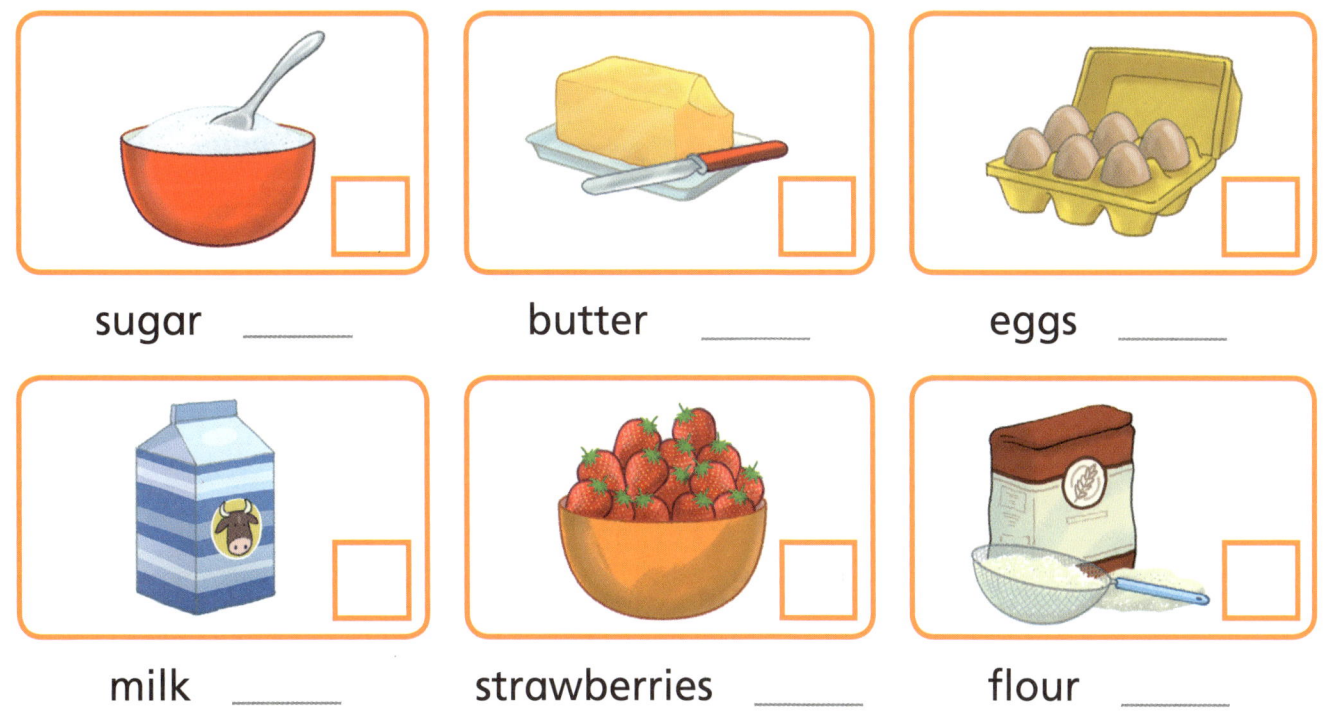

sugar ____   butter ____   eggs ____

milk ____   strawberries ____   flour ____

3 💬 Communicate Listen and repeat. 🔊 50 Draw. Act out with your friend.

This is my new machine. It's a sandwich machine!

Great idea!

3, 2, 1 …!

Literacy reading a story

2 Lesson 8 Communication

Rooftops Skills

Listen and Speak

1 Listen and tick ✓ or cross ✗. 🔊 51 💬 **Communicate** Say.

2 Make your communication cards.  CB page 93

3 🔗 **Collaborate** Say and play.

Life skills

Rooftops Round Up

Lesson 9 Round Up **2**

Song 🎵

1 Listen and point. 🔊 53 Listen and sing. 🔊 53

2 Read and write **N** for or **A** for .

☐ catch ☐ bike shed ☐ gym ☐ draw
☐ ride a bike ☐ climb ☐ play football

3 💡 Be creative   Listen and read. 🔊 54 Draw and write. Share.

This is my friend Nizzy.
He's in the classroom.
He can write.

My Amazing friend!

This is _____.

He's / She's in the _____.

He / She can _____.

Life skills 25

I can do it!

Anna ✓

Tommy ✓

Neena ✗

1 Throw the dice. Go around the board and say.
2 When you land on an image with a green tick, say your I can sentences.
3 The first person to say all their I can sentences is the winner.

You need

Review game 1

I can

Oscar ✗

Nizzy ✓

I can

Project 1

Rooftops Project

The Project
Make the school game.

Watch the video.

Stage 1: Think!

Remember the game. Where are the children? Say.

Sam is in the ...

Write.   bike shed   gym   toilets   classroom   playground

1 _____   2 _____   3 _____

4 _____   5 _____

Life skills

You need

Project 1

Stage 2: Plan and prepare

1. Work in a group. Think. What's in your school?

2. Draw the places in your school.

3. Draw and colour a child. Write the name.

4. Put your children in the school. Look and remember.

Stage 3: Play!

Turn around. Where's Ali?

I can't remember!

He's in the classroom!

Here's a clue. He can read.

Lesson 2 Song and Grammar **3**

1 Listen and sing. 🔊59 Listen and number. 🔊60 Write.

Song 🎵

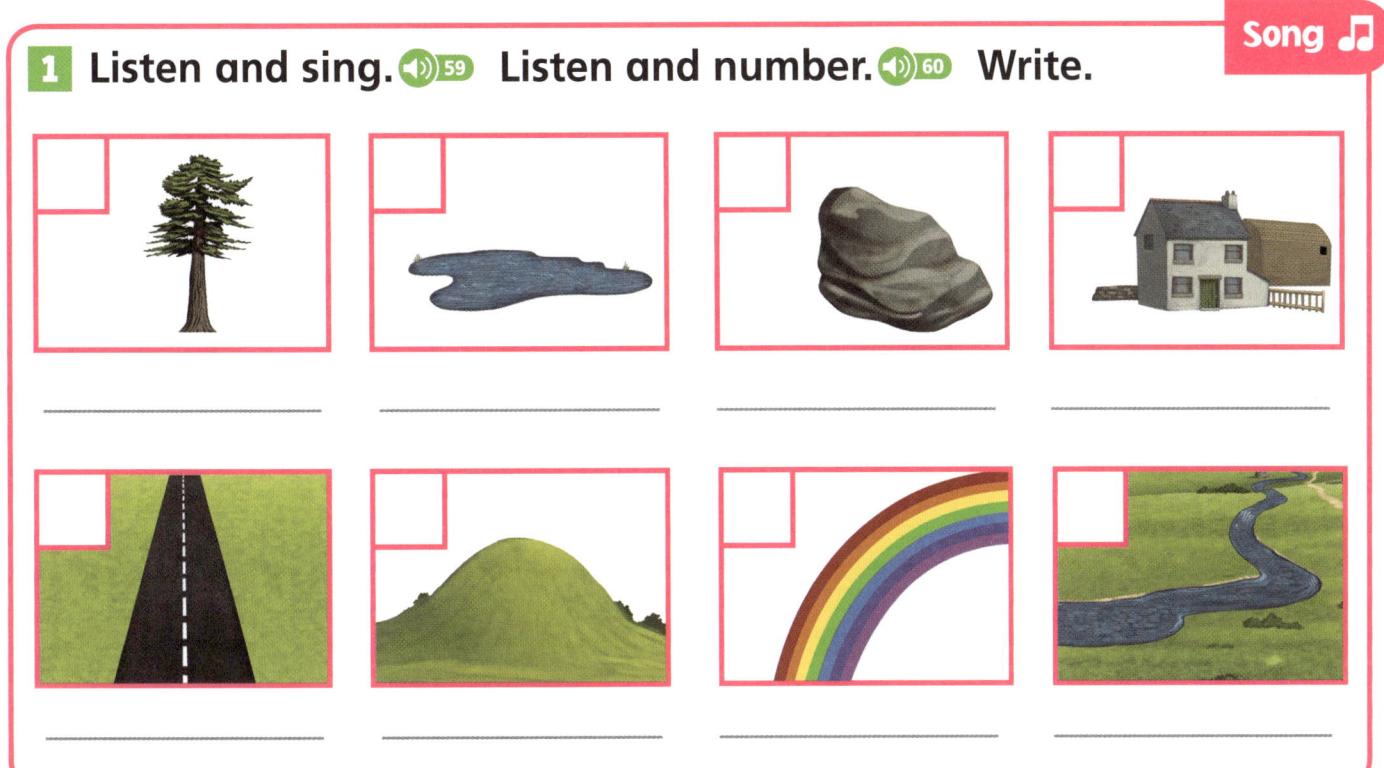

2 Look and read. Write *A* or *B*. **3** 💬 Communicate Say and play.

☐ farm   ☐ lake   ☐ river   ☐ rock
☐ hill   ☐ rainbow   ☐ road   ☐ tree

Can you see a tree?
Yes, I can.
Picture B.

Can you see a …? Yes, I can. / No, I can't.   31

3 In the countryside

Lesson 3 Culture

1 Look and say the places. Write.

2 Listen and number. 🔊 61

farm   hill   river   road

3 Make a mini-book. **AB** 💬 **Communicate** Show and tell.

My favourite place is the lake.

I can see a tree.

32 Life skills

Lesson 4 Everyday language and Values **3**

1 Listen and point. 🔊 63 Listen and repeat. 🔊 63

2 Listen and number. 🔊 64 Write.

over   Excuse   Where's   me

Excuse _____.

It's _____ there.

_____ the party?

_____ me.

3 💬 Communicate Act out with your friend.

Excuse me. Where's the farm, please?

It's over there.

Our Values

Are you polite and helpful?

Life skills 33

3 Lesson 5 Story

The nature reserve

1 Listen and follow the story. 🔊 65

2 🔄 Review Find, circle and write. 💬 Communicate Say.

d _____   c _____   f _____   f _____

3 Listen and repeat. 🔊 66   💭 Think Colour and say.

I think the story is …

3 Lesson 6 Vocabulary and Grammar

1 Listen, point and repeat. 🔊 67 Listen and say the word. 🔊 68

1. hedgehog 2. deer 3. owl

4. fox 5. spider

2 Listen and say the number. 🔊 69 Listen and repeat. 🔊 69

3 💬 Communicate Play.

It's next to the tree!

Number 3! The hedgehog!

1 2 3 4 5

36 | **Vocabulary** forest animals | It's behind / in front of / next to …

Rooftops Book Club

Lesson 7 Literacy 3

1 What happens next? Guess and tick ✓.

The cake machine makes ...

☐ A pink and yellow cake. ☐ A small, black cake. ☐ A big, pink cake.

2 📖 page 8 and 9 🔊 70 Order and write.   cake   red   new   can't

| We _____ eat this! | A big, _____ cake. | Let's make a _____ cake. | A _____ comes out. |

3 💬 **Communicate** Listen and repeat. 🔊 71 Play *What's in the cake?*

What's in the cake?

OK! Eggs! Your turn.

Eggs and milk.

Literacy reading a story

Lesson 8 Communication

Rooftops Skills

Listen and Speak

1 Listen and number. 🔊 72 Match. 💬 Communicate Say.

1 The owl is — behind the tree.
2 The fox is — in front of the rock.
3 The hedgehog is — next to the lake.
4 The deer is — next to the tree.

2 Make your communication cards. **CB page 91**

3 🔗 Collaborate Say and play.

"OK. Can you see a hedgehog?"

"Yes, I can. It's next to the tree."

Life skills

Rooftops Round Up

Lesson 9 Round Up 3

Song 🎵

1 Listen and point. 🔊 74 Listen and sing. 🔊 74

2 Read and circle.

1 It's behind the tree.
   deer / fox

2 It's in front of the tree.
   spider / hedgehog

3 It's next to the tree.
   owl / fox

3 💡 Be creative Listen and read. 🔊 75 Draw and write. Share.

Can you see a spider?
It's in front of the rock.
It's small and black.

Amazing wildlife!

Can you see a _____?

It's _____.

It's _____.

Life skills 39

Lesson 1 Vocabulary

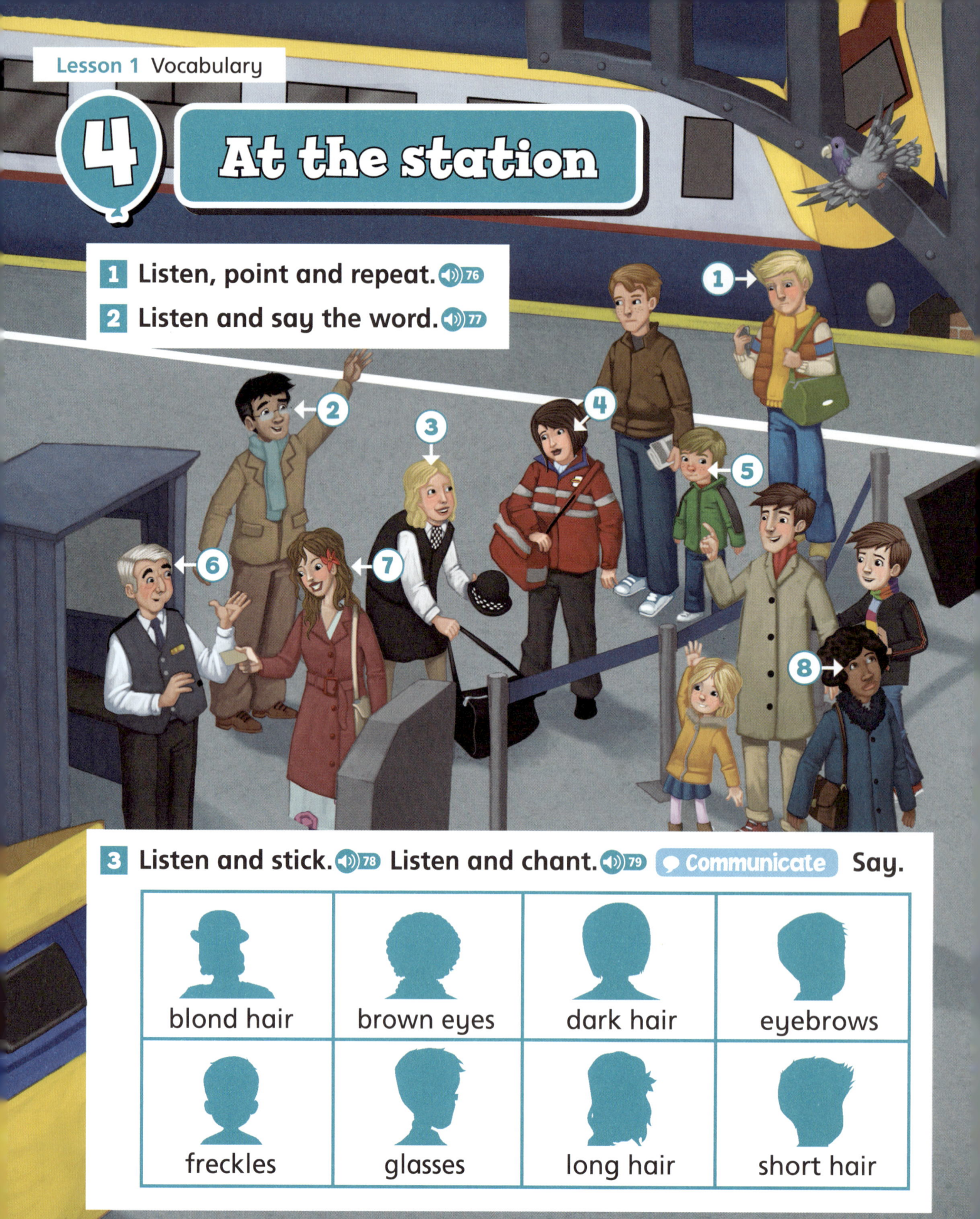

4 At the station

1 Listen, point and repeat. 🔊 76
2 Listen and say the word. 🔊 77

3 Listen and stick. 🔊 78 Listen and chant. 🔊 79 💬 Communicate Say.

| blond hair | brown eyes | dark hair | eyebrows |
| freckles | glasses | long hair | short hair |

40 Vocabulary how we look

Lesson 2 Song and Grammar 4

1 Listen and sing. 🔊 80 Listen and number. 🔊 81 Write.   Song 🎵

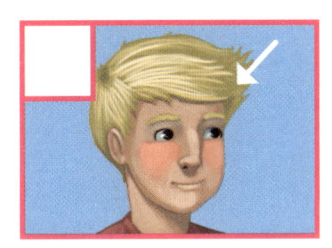

2 Circle the odd one out. Tick ✓. **3** 💬 Communicate Say and play.

short hair ☐
glasses ☐

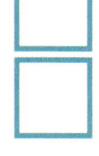

freckles ☐
brown eyes ☐

blond hair ☐
long hair ☐

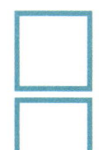

She's got glasses.
This one!

He's / She's got …
41

4 Lesson 3 Culture — The train museum

1. **Look and say. Write.**
2. **Listen and number.** 🔊 82

blond hair   short hair
glasses   freckles

He's got _____.

I've got _____.

He's got _____.

She's got _____.

3. **Make a mini-book.** AB 💬 Communicate **Show and tell.**

"I've got blue eyes and blond hair."

"I've got dark hair!"

42 Life skills

Lesson 4 Everyday language and Values **4**

1 Listen and point. 🔊83 Listen and repeat. 🔊83

- Hello, I'm Emily.
- Hello, Emily. Nice to meet you.
- Nice to meet you, too.

2 Listen and write the names. 🔊84

Alex   Rosa   Chris   Stacey

1. Grandma _____
2. Mr Black _____
3. _____ Dad
4. Mrs Green _____

3 💬 Communicate Act out with your friend.

- Hello. I'm Mark.
- Hello, Mark. Nice to meet you.
- Nice to meet you, too.

Our Values

Are you polite to adults?

Life skills 43

4 Lesson 5 Story

Uncle Brian's visit

1 Listen and follow the story. 🔊 85

1 Look at all the people.
Where's Uncle Brian?
I can't see Uncle Brian.

2 Look, I've got a photo. This is Uncle Brian.
Is this you, Dad?

3 Yes, it is. I'm wearing a cap. Uncle Brian is wearing a red T-shirt and brown shorts.
OK. Let's look for Uncle Brian.

4 Look! I can see him! He's wearing a blue coat.
No, it isn't Uncle Brian. He's got short hair now.

5 Look! There he is! He's got short hair and freckles. He's wearing a green scarf.
No, it isn't Uncle Brian. He's got glasses now.

6 I can see him! He's got short hair, freckles and glasses.
He's wearing jeans and boots.

44 Literacy understanding a story

7 No, no. That isn't Brian.
Dad! This photo is no good. It's old.

8 I can see him! Brian!

9 Here's Uncle Brian. He's wearing a red T-shirt and brown shorts!

10 Hello, Uncle Brian. Nice to meet you.
Uncle Brian, here's my scarf. It's cold!
Thank you, Oscar. It's summer in Australia!

2 🔄 **Review** Find, circle and write. 💬 **Communicate** Say.

r _____   s _____   l _____   t _____

3 Listen and repeat. 🔊 86   💭 **Think** Colour and say.

I think the story is ...

Lesson 6 Vocabulary and Grammar

1 Listen, point and repeat. 🔊 87   Listen and say the word. 🔊 88

1. coat
2. scarf
3. jeans
4. shorts
5. boots

2 Listen and say the number. 🔊 89   Listen and repeat. 🔊 89

3 💬 Communicate Play.

He's wearing jeans and a yellow scarf.

Number 3!

Vocabulary clothes   He's / She's wearing …

Rooftops Book Club

Lesson 7 Literacy **4**

1 What happens next? Guess and tick ✓.

The cake is very good. ☐   The cake isn't very good. ☐

2 📖 page 10 and 11 🔊 90 Read, write and number.

Where   cake   1

1. _____ is it?

2. 3, 2, _____.

3. Here's the _____.

3 💬 Communicate Listen and repeat. 🔊 91 Act out with your friend.

3, 2, 1 …

Where is it?

Here's the cake.

Literacy reading a story   47

4 Lesson 8 Communication

Rooftops Skills

Listen and Speak

1 Listen and number. 🔊 92 Read and number. 💬 **Communicate** Say.

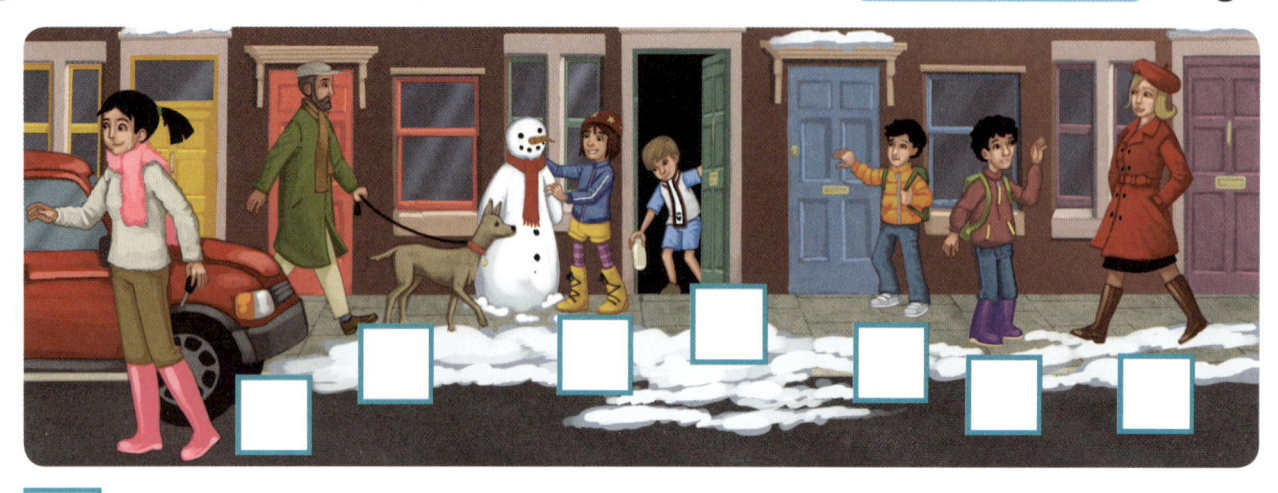

☐ She's got short hair. She's wearing yellow shorts.

☐ He's got dark hair. He's wearing purple boots.

☐ She's got blond hair. She's wearing a red coat.

☐ She's got long hair. She's wearing a pink scarf.

2 Make your communication cards. **CB page 91**

3 **Collaborate** Say and play.

Here's Mr Delfosse. He's wearing a green coat.

Oh! That's different. He's wearing a black coat.

Life skills

Rooftops Round Up

Lesson 9 Round Up **4**

Song 🎵

1 Listen and point. 🔊 94 Listen and sing. 🔊 94

2 Read and write the names.

1 She's got freckles and blond hair. _____

2 He's wearing boots and blue jeans. _____

3 💡 Be creative Listen and read. 🔊 95 Draw and write. Share.

She's got short hair. She's wearing a red coat and a pink scarf. Who is it?

An amazing disguise!

She's / He's got _____.

She's / He's wearing _____

_____. Who is it?

Life skills

An amazing walk

START

Anna

?

You're tired!
Go back 2.

?

It's sunny!
Go forward 2.

Oscar

?

?

It's windy!
Go back 2.

Neena

?

50

You need

Review game 2

It's rainy.
Miss a turn.

You can run!
Nizzy

Go forward 2.

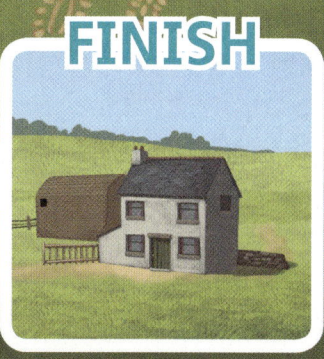

Miss the bus.
Miss a turn.

?

Mum

Picnic stop!
Miss a turn.

FINISH

Project 2 — Rooftops Project

The Project
Make a funny flip book.

Watch the video.

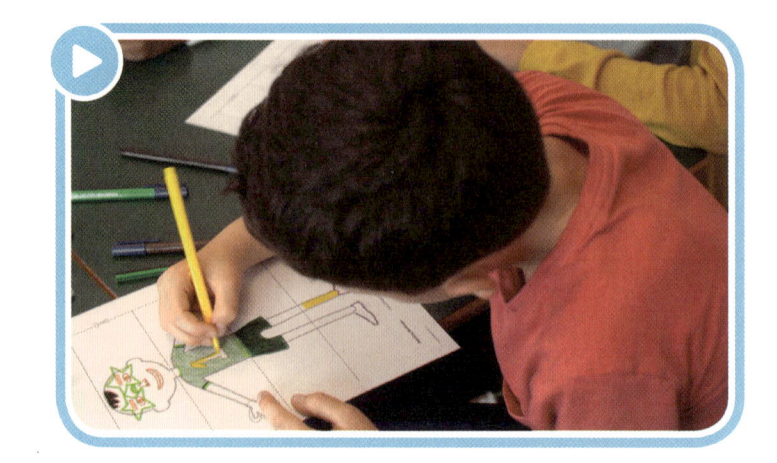

Stage 1: Think!

Think and match the parts to the pictures.

Write the words.

jeans   blond hair   boots   T-shirt

1 _____   2 _____   3 _____   4 _____

52 Life skills

You need

Project 2

Stage 2: Plan and prepare

1 Work in a group. Think of characters for your flip book.

2 Draw and colour.

3 Staple your pictures together to make a book.

4 Cut along the lines. Be careful.

Stage 3: Play!

It's my turn. Look. He's got short hair and glasses.

He's wearing a pink scarf and yellow boots. You're next.

Lesson 1 Vocabulary

5 At the farm

1. Listen, point and repeat. 🔊 96
2. Listen and say the word. 🔊 97

3. Listen and stick. 🔊 98   Listen and chant. 🔊 99   💬 Communicate   Say.

| bee | chicken | cow | donkey |
| duck | goat | pig | sheep |

54   **Vocabulary** farm animals

Lesson 2 Song and Grammar 5

1 Listen and sing. 🔊 100 Listen and number. 🔊 101 Write. Song 🎵

2 What's on your farm? Write. **3** 💬 Communicate Say, play and write.

pig(s)   chicken(s)   bee(s)   donkey(s)   cow(s)   duck(s)   goat(s)

My farm

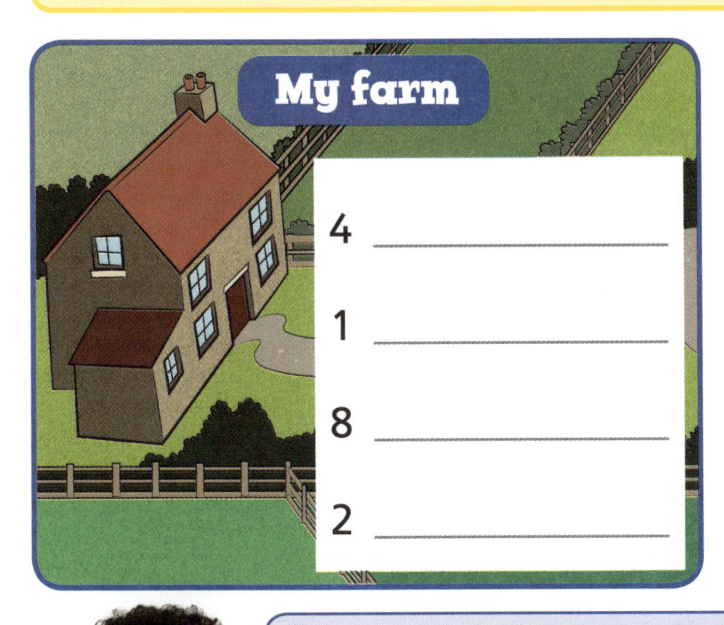

4 _____
1 _____
8 _____
2 _____

My friend's farm

4 _____
1 _____
8 _____
2 _____

On my farm there are 4 cows.

4 cows. OK. On my farm there's a donkey.

There's a / There are 2 … 55

5 A farm visit

Lesson 3 Culture

1. **Look and say the animals. Write.**
2. **Listen and number.** 🔊 102

goat   sheep   chickens   cows

There's a  _____.   There's a _____.

There are 5  _____.   There are 3 _____.

3. **Make a mini-book.** AB 💬 Communicate **Show and tell.**

There's a cow. It's black and white.

1, 2, 3 ... There are 3 ducks.

56 Life skills

Lesson 4 Everyday language and Values **5**

1 Listen and point. 🔊 104   Listen and repeat. 🔊 104

How many tickets?

3 tickets, please.

2 Listen and number. 🔊 105   Write.

___4___ tickets, please.

_____ tickets, please.

_____ tickets, please.

_____ tickets, please.

3 💬 Communicate   Act out with your friend.

How many tickets?

3 tickets, please.

Our Values

Do you follow the country code?

Life skills   57

5 Lesson 5 Story

The mysterious animal

1 Listen and follow the story. 🔊 106

1 I'm hot! Let's have an ice cream.

Come on, Neena!

2 There's a mysterious animal in the barn!

3 It's got big ears!

Is it a donkey? Look! It's got big ears.

4 No. It's small! It's got small feet and big ears.

Is it a mouse?

5 No, it isn't a mouse! It hasn't got teeth. It's got wings.

6 Is it a chicken?

No, it isn't a chicken. It's got ears.

58 **Literacy** understanding a story

7 It's got big eyes and it's got brown feathers!

It's an owl!

8 Look. This is an owl. It's got big ears and small feet. It's got wings and feathers. It hasn't got teeth.

Yes, there's one in the barn. It's small.

9 It's a baby owl. It's hungry.

10 Thank you, Neena. This is for you.

Come back and visit us soon.

2 🔄 **Review** Find, circle and write. 💬 **Communicate** Say.

b _____   j _____   a _____   o _____

3 Listen and repeat. 🔊 107   💭 **Think** Colour and say.

I think the story is …

5 Lesson 6 Vocabulary and Grammar

1 Listen, point and repeat. 🔊 108 Listen and say the word. 🔊 109

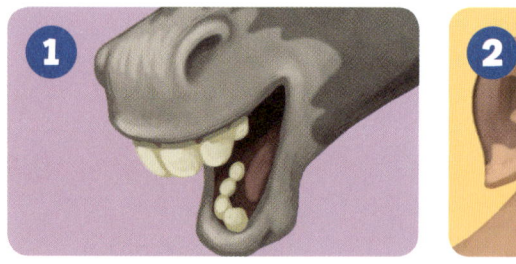

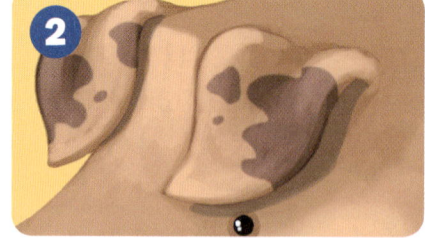

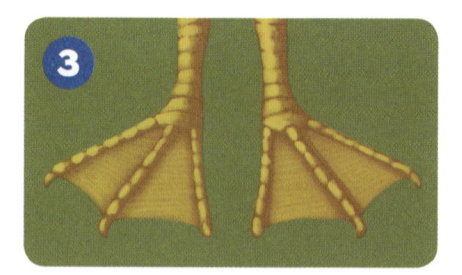

1. teeth
2. ears
3. feet
4. feathers
5. wings

2 Listen and say the number. 🔊 110 Listen and repeat. 🔊 110

3 💬 Communicate Play.

It's got big yellow feet.
It hasn't got feathers.

Number 4!
The frog!

1. 2. 3. 4. 5. 6.

60 | **Vocabulary** animal body parts | It's got … / It hasn't got …

Rooftops Book Club

Lesson 7 Literacy 5

1 Who's happy? Guess and tick ✔. Say.

- Mum ☐
- Clunk ☐
- Ben ☐
- Rosie ☐
- Grandpa ☐

2 📖 page 12 and 13 🔊 111 Read and tick ✔ or cross ✘.

1. Rosie, Ben and Grandpa go to a café. ☐
2. Mum, Rosie and Ben eat a big, red cake. ☐
3. Clunk says 'I don't like this cake!' ☐
4. Everyone is happy! ☐

3 💬 Communicate Listen and repeat. 🔊 112 Draw. Act out with your friend.

Do you like this cake?

Yes, I do.

Literacy reading a story 61

5 Lesson 8 Communication

Rooftops Skills

Listen and Speak

1 Listen and circle *Yes* or *No*. 🔊 113   💬 **Communicate** Look and say.

1	Yes	No
2	Yes	No
3	Yes	No
4	Yes	No
5	Yes	No
6	Yes	No

2 Make your communication cards. **CB page 89**

3 🤝 **Collaborate** Say and play.

"There are 4 cows."

"Oh, that's different. There are 3 cows in my picture."

62 Life skills

Rooftops Round Up

Lesson 9 Round Up 5

Song 🎵

1 Listen and point. 🔊 115   Listen and sing. 🔊 115

2 Read and write *A* or *B*.

A

B

It's got feathers. ☐	It's got big ears. ☐
It hasn't got wings. ☐	It's got small ears. ☐
It's got 4 feet. ☐	It hasn't got teeth. ☐

3 💡 Be creative   Listen and read. 🔊 116   Draw and write. Share.

It's got feathers.
It hasn't got teeth.
It's a chicken.

An amazing animal!

✔ _____.

✘ _____.

It's a _____.

Life skills | 63

Lesson 1 Vocabulary

6 At the fair

1 Listen, point and repeat. 🔊 117

2 Listen and say the word. 🔊 118

3 Listen and stick. 🔊 119 Listen and chant. 🔊 120 💬 Communicate Say.

juice	lemonade	milk	pasta
pizza	popcorn	salad	soup

64 **Vocabulary** food and drink

Lesson 2 Song and Grammar 6

Song 🎵

1 Listen and sing. 🔊 121 Listen and number. 🔊 122 Write.

2 Look, read and number.   **3** 💬 Communicate Mime, say and play.

I'm eating pasta.
I'm drinking lemonade. ☐

I'm eating popcorn.
I'm drinking milk. ☐

I'm eating soup.
I'm drinking juice. ☐

I'm eating salad.
I'm drinking juice. ☐

What are you eating?

I'm eating soup.

What are you drinking / eating?
I'm drinking / eating …

65

6 Lesson 3 Culture — At the fair

1 Look and say the food and drink. Write.

2 Listen and number. 🔊 123

pasta   salad
lemonade   juice

I'm eating _____.

He's drinking _____.

He's eating _____.

He's drinking _____.

3 Make a mini-book. **AB** 💬 **Communicate** Show and tell.

What are you eating?

I'm eating pasta. My favourite food is pasta!

Life skills

Lesson 4 Everyday language and Values 6

1 Listen and point. 🔊 124 Listen and repeat. 🔊 124

Hello.
I'd like some popcorn, please.

Here you are.
Thank you.

2 Listen and number. 🔊 125 Write.

juice   milk   pasta   salad

I'd like some _____, please.

I'd like some _____, please.

I'd like some _____, please.

I'd like some _____, please.

3 💬 Communicate Act out with your friend.

I'd like some pasta, please.
Here you are.
Thank you.

Our Values

Do you recycle?

Life skills 67

Lesson 5 Story

Are you ready?

1 Listen and follow the story. 🔊 126

1 Come on, Nizzy. It's the show today! Are you ready?
Oh, er …

2 Nizzy! Look at my wings! I love dressing up!
Oh. I don't like dressing up.

3 Hi, Nizzy. Listen. I like playing music!
Oh. Er … I don't like playing music.

4 I like acting. It's fun!

5 Oh … I don't like acting.

6 Oh, dear! I can't dance. I can't sing. I don't want to be in the show.

68 Literacy understanding a story

7. Hello, Nizzy! Can you help me?
Yes … I like painting!

8. This is fun. I like making posters!
Come on, Nizzy! Let's go!

9. Thank you, Nizzy.
It's time for the show.

10. Thank you! Thank you! And thanks to Nizzy and TJ, too!
I like helping!

2 Review **Find, circle and write.** Communicate **Say.**

r _____   s _____   d _____   s _____

3 Listen and repeat. 127   Think **Colour and say.**

I think the story is …

6 Lesson 6 Vocabulary and Grammar

1 Listen, point and repeat. 🔊 128   Listen and say the word. 🔊 129

1. dressing up
2. acting 
3. playing music 
4. painting 
5. making posters 

2 Listen and say the number. 🔊 130   Listen and repeat. 🔊 130

3 💬 Communicate   Play.

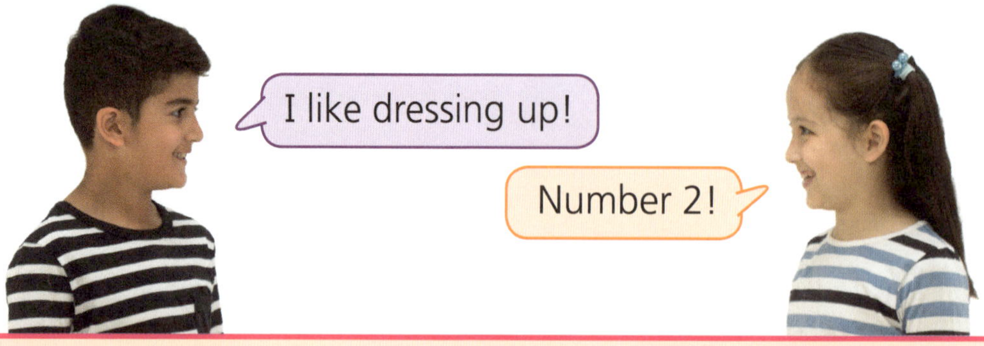

I like dressing up!

Number 2!

Vocabulary activities   I like / don't like (acting).

Rooftops Book Club

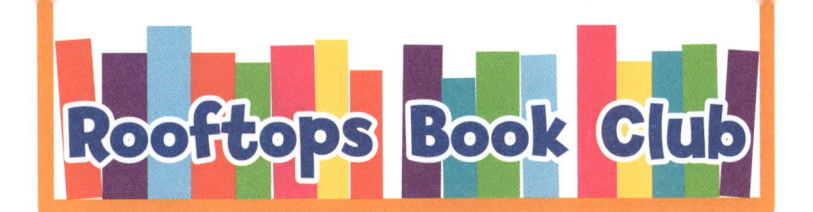

Lesson 7 Literacy 6

1 Remember. Order the pictures. Tell the story.

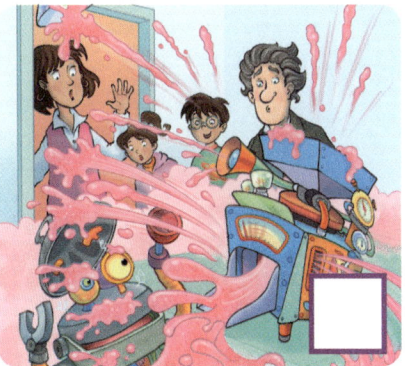

2 📖 page 4 to 13 Read your reader. 🔊 131 Match.

1 Grandpa, Rosie, Ben and Clunk   a small, black cake.

2 Grandpa has got a   are in the kitchen.

3 First, the cake machine makes   new cake machine!

4 Grandpa wants   a big, pink mess!

5 Then, the cake machine makes   a big, red cake.

3 💬 Communicate Work in groups. Act out the play!

Grandpa puts in eggs. Clunk puts in strawberries.

Literacy reading a story

6 Lesson 8 Communication

Rooftops Skills

Listen and Speak

1 Listen and draw ☺ or ☹. 🔊 132 Write *like* or *don't like*.

💬 **Communicate** Say.

1 I _____ dressing up.

2 I _____ eating pasta.

3 I _____ playing music.

4 I _____ tomato soup.

5 I _____ orange juice.

2 Make your communication cards. **CB page 89**

3 🔗 **Collaborate** Say and play.

I like dressing up. And you?

Me, too! I like dressing up, too!

Life skills

Rooftops Round Up

Lesson 9 Round Up 6

Song 🎵

1 Listen and point. 🔊 134 Listen and sing. 🔊 134

2 Read and write the names.

I'm eating popcorn. _____   I'm drinking juice. _____

I like playing music. _____   I like dressing up. _____

3 💡 Be creative   Listen and read. 🔊 135   Draw and write. Share.

My amazing skills!

I like making posters. I can draw and write!

I like _____.

I can _____.

Life skills 73

The Speak Up Game

START
- speak!
- sing and do!
- whisper!
- shout!

FINISH

What's your favourite food?

You need

Review game 3

Ask a question. Do you like ... ?

How old are you?

Have you got brothers and sisters?

Project 3 — Rooftops Project

The Project
Write and perform a poem.

Watch the video.

Stage 1: Think

Remember the poem. Choose and write.

big   playing music   soup   blue   feathers

I'm an amazing animal!

I've got _____ feet.

I like _____ .

And _____ to eat!

It's an amazing animal!

It's got _____ wings.

It's got purple _____ .

Listen! How it sings!

Our amazing animal

I'm an amazing animal!
I've got _big_ feet.
I like _playing music_.
And _soup_ to eat!

It's an amazing animal!
It's got _blue_ wings.
It's got _purple feathers_.
Listen! How it sings!

Which other words match the gaps? Why? Colour the boxes.

(dressing up) (popcorn) (teeth) (green) (making posters) (ears)

(small) (pasta) (legs) (yellow) (playing football) (salad)

Life skills

You need

Project 3

Stage 2: Plan and prepare

1 Work in a group. Choose words to complete the poem.

2 Make some costumes for your poem performance.

3 Choose some actions for your poem performance.

4 Practice your poem with your friends.

Stage 3: Perform

I've got big, green feet.

I'm an amazing animal.

77

Happy Halloween

1 Listen, point and repeat. 🔊 136 **2** Listen and chant. 🔊 137
3 Listen and say the word. 🔊 138

1. cobwebs
2. wizard
3. spider
4. fairy
5. skeleton
6. troll

4 Look and number. Write.   **5** 💬 Communicate Say.

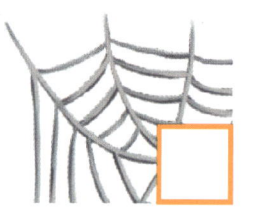

Can you see a fairy?

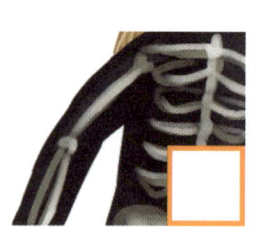

Vocabulary Halloween

Merry Christmas

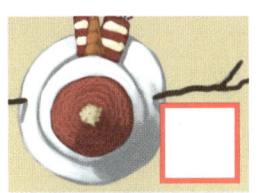

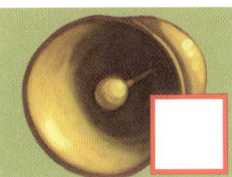

1 Listen, point and repeat. 🔊 139
2 Listen and sing. 🔊 140
3 Listen and say the word. 🔊 141

Song 🎵

1. reindeer
2. Father Christmas
3. chimney
4. light
5. snowman
6. bell

4 Look and number. Write.

5 💬 Communicate — Say.

This is a …

Vocabulary Christmas

Happy Easter

1 Listen, point and repeat. 🔊 142
2 Listen and chant. 🔊 143
3 Listen and say the word. 🔊 144

1. milk
2. raisins
3. flour
4. sugar
5. spice
6. butter

4 Complete the recipe. **5** 💬 Communicate Say.

Hot Cross Buns

Do you like milk?

80 **Vocabulary** Easter

Picture Dictionary **1**

1 Write.   garden   bathroom   kitchen   living room
dining room   garage   bedroom   hall

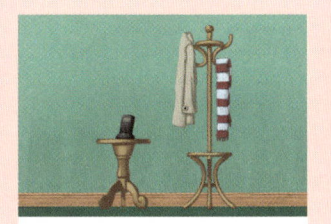

_____   _____   _____   _____

_____   _____   _____   _____

2 Write.   bath   bed   sofa   cupboard   table

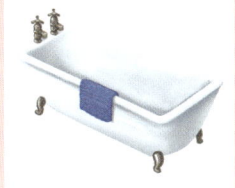

_____   _____   _____   _____   _____

My amazing progress

3 Look and tick ✓ your favourite activities in Unit 1.

2 Picture Dictionary

1 Write.   ride a bike   write   climb   draw   catch   play football   read   hop

2 Write.   playground   gym   toilets   bike shed   classroom

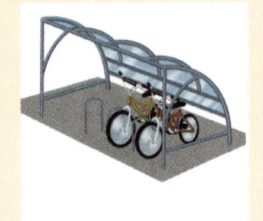

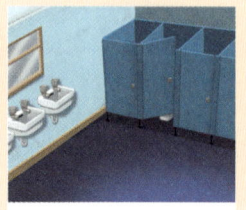

My amazing progress

3 Look and tick ✓ your favourite activities in Unit 2.

Picture Dictionary 3

1 Write. | rock lake river tree road
farm hill rainbow

2 Write. | hedgehog fox spider owl deer

My amazing progress

3 Look and tick ✓ your favourite activities in Unit 3.

83

4 Picture Dictionary

1 Write.

| glasses | brown eyes | dark hair | short hair |
| eyebrows | freckles | blond hair | long hair |

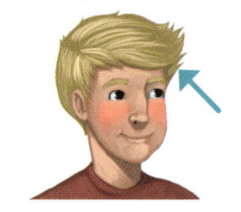

2 Write.

scarf   jeans   boots   shorts   coat

My amazing progress

3 Look and tick ✓ your favourite activities in Unit 4.

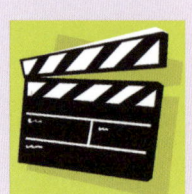

84

Picture Dictionary 5

1 Write.

> bee   pig   sheep   cow
> donkey   chicken   duck   goat

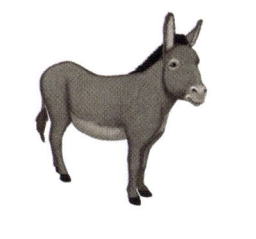

_____   _____   _____   _____

_____   _____   _____   _____

2 Write.

> teeth   ears   wings   feet   feathers

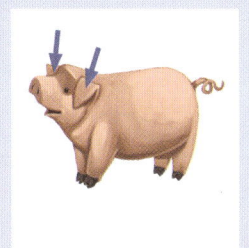

_____   _____   _____   _____   _____

My amazing progress

3 Look and tick ✔ your favourite activities in Unit 5.

85

6 Picture Dictionary

1 Write.

salad   pizza   milk   pasta
soup   juice   lemonade   popcorn

_____   _____   _____   _____

_____   _____   _____   _____

2 Write.

dressing up   acting   playing music
painting   making posters

_____   _____   _____   _____   _____

My amazing progress

3 Look and tick ✓ your favourite activities in Unit 6.

My Progress

Project 1–3 Self Evaluation

1 🗨 Think Look and draw 😊, 😐 or ☹. Colour.

Project 1

My effort ☆ ☆ ☆

I know Unit 1 and Unit 2 words.

Project 2

My effort ☆ ☆ ☆

I know Unit 3 and Unit 4 words.

Project 3

My effort ☆ ☆ ☆

I know Unit 5 and Unit 6 words.

Cut outs

Contents

Communication cards Unit 5 & 6   89

Communication cards Unit 3 & 4   91

Communication cards Unit 1 & 2   93

Finger puppets   95

Key

✂ ----- cut

🖍 glue

———— fold

💬 **Communicate** Talk about the picture. Find 9 differences.

A

💬 **Communicate** Ask and answer in groups. Colour 🙂. — Do you like … ?

Communication cards 5 and 6

89

Communicate Talk about the picture. Find 9 differences.

B

⑤

Communicate **Collaborate** Agree 2 foods and 2 activities for your picnic. Write.

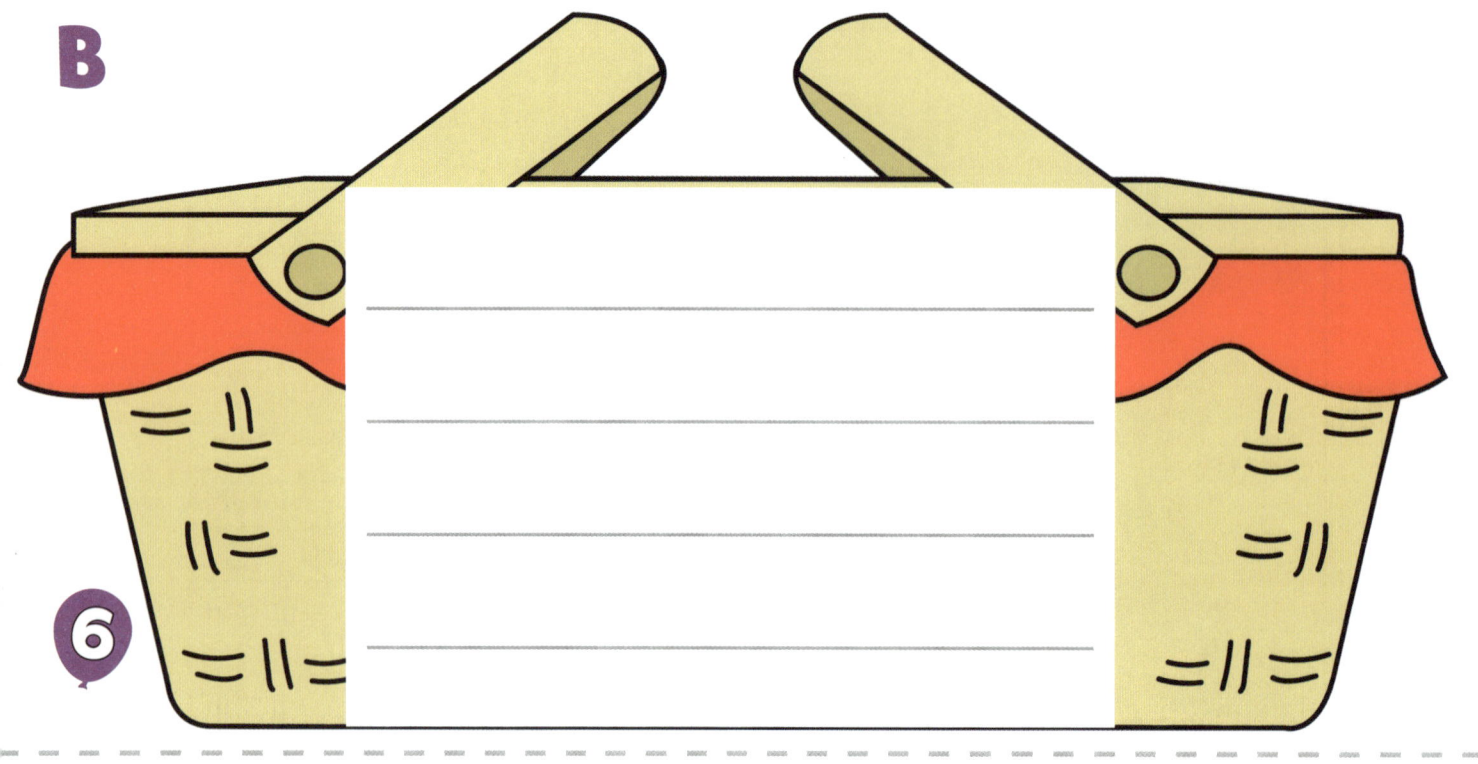

B

⑥

90 Communication cards ⑤ and ⑥

Draw.  **Communicate** Ask, answer and draw.

A

Communicate Talk about the picture. Find 9 differences.

A

Communication cards ③ and ④

91

Draw. 🦌 🦔 🕷 🐱   💬 Communicate Ask, answer and draw.

💬 Communicate Talk about the picture. Circle 9 differences.

92   Communication cards ③ and ④

Communicate Ask and answer.

A

Where's …
- Mum?
- Uncle?
- Oscar?
- Kitty?

1

Communicate Talk about the picture. Find 7 differences.

A

2

Communication cards **1** and **2**

93

Communicate Ask and answer.

B

Where's …
Anna?
Dad?
Grandpa?
Grandma?

1

Communicate Talk about the picture. Circle 7 differences.

B

2

94   Communication cards 1 and 2

Finger puppets S Cut Stick Fold 95

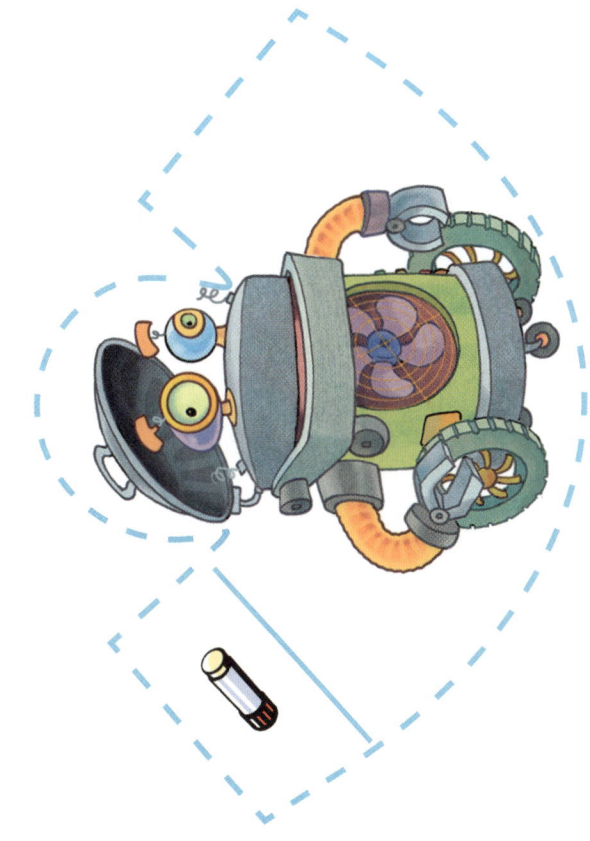

96

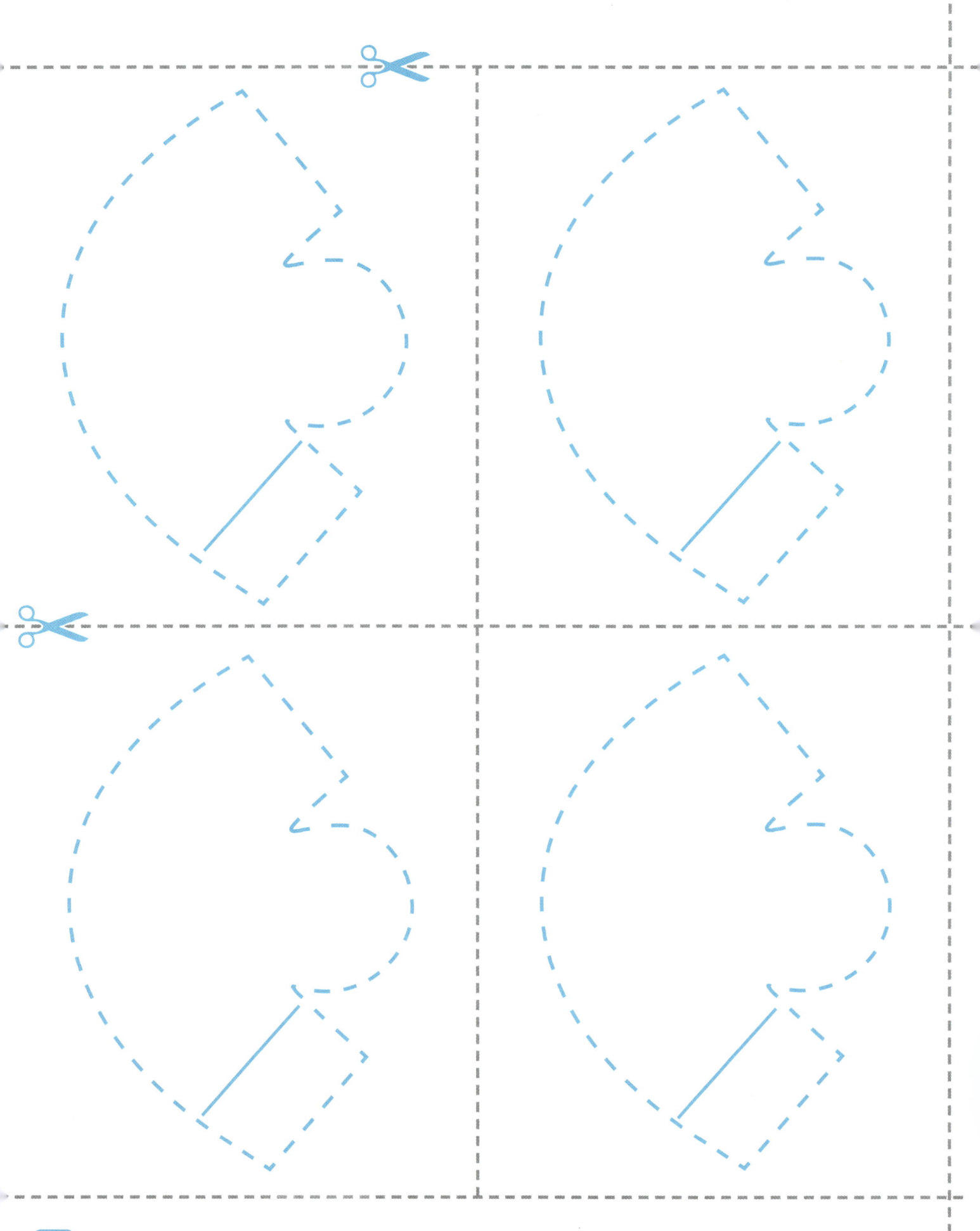

1

garden	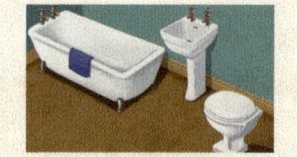 bathroom	 kitchen	 living room
 dining room	 garage	 bedroom	 hall

2

ride a bike	 write	 climb	 draw
 catch	 play football	 read	 hop

3

rock	 lake	 river	 tree
 road	 farm	 hill	 rainbow